G000147661

Ma,
We hope this book will
help in your travel planning.
We look forward to seeing
you here!

All our love,
Martha + Pat + Toula.

Discovering

California

Discovering

California

Text: L. P. Linebaugh
Concept and Design: Robert D. Shangle

First Printing October, 2000
American Products Publishing Company
Division of American Products Corporation
6750 SW 111th Avenue, Beaverton, Oregon 97008-5389

"Learn about America in a beautiful way."

Library of Congress Cataloging-in-Publication Data

Linebaugh, L. P., 1964-
   Discovering California / text: L. P. Linebaugh; concept and design: Robert D. Shangle, publisher.
      p. cm.
   ISBN 1-884958-56-7 – ISBN 1-884958-55-9 (pbk)
   1. California—Pictorial works. 2. California—Description and travel. 3.
California—History. I. Shangle, Robert D. II. Title.

F862.L596 2000
917.94—dc21   00-061825

Copyright © 2000 by Robert D. Shangle
Printed in Hong Kong
Concept, Publishing and Distribution by
American Products Publlishing Company
Beaverton, Oregon U.S.A.

Contents

Introduction

Beauty is in the eye of the beholder. Beauty is also in variety. These are two aspects of an idea that seems very appropriate when we talk about California. If we could command a hundred or a thousand Californians to appear before us and give us their individual notions of the state's glories, we'd receive at least a thousand different responses.

Because California is so big, it has some built-in differences. Its latitudinal range is vast — from 32° in the south to 42° in the north. Its long reach accounts for about a thousand miles of the continent's Pacific edge. As a result, its climates can never be spoken of in the singular. Add to that all the mountain chains of California that control weather from west to east, and the climatic variations increase. So the north coast Californian and the south coast Californian are accustomed to different weather regimes. So is the San Diego dweller and the Imperial Valley farmer, although they inhabit the same latitude only 80-miles apart.

Another complication arises because there are so many dissimilar landscapes. The state could be divided into a thousand little principalities, all very distinct, and each an embodiment of the beauty of California. If we look at a map that is big enough to show what is there, it would be as an introduction to a feast, where the courses are endless. To begin our journey the eye might take pleasure in roaming along the corrugated coastline, somehow tied together by the big *bow* the middle of the range known as San Francisco Bay. Gaze at the northern interior and become lost in the jumbled mass of mountain systems: the Coast Range, the Siskiyou, Marble, Salmon, Trinity, and Cascade Range, and over in the northeastern corner, locate the WarnerCascade Range, and over in the northeastern corner, locate the Warner Mountains. Look at Mt. Shasta that reaches an elevation of 14,162 feet and envision the glacial beauty in your mind's eye. Not quite California's tallest mountain, certainly Mt. Shasta the most theatrical.

The biggest mountain range in California dominates everything north to south. Run our finger over the long shaded part of the map overprinted in bold letters: Sierra Nevada, one of the world's natural wonders. It is a fault-block mountain system of such mighty mass that it rivals the Pacific Ocean in determining how the weather will effect life as it is lived in California. The map shows the monumental glacial valleys and lakes of the Range. And over on the east and southeast are enormous desert areas that are largely the Sierra's creations. Colored in buff-white and-tan hues, the deserts include the eastern valleys, culminating in Death Valley, the Mojave and Colorado deserts. In the middle of the triangular basin that is identified as the Colorado Desert, there is that outsized oddity known as the Salton Sea. This enormous accidental lake was created in 1905 by Colorado River floodwaters after a somewhat experimental irrigation project got out of control.

There is so much in California that declares certain greatness, and it does not have to be the biggest, tallest, oldest, youngest, driest, wettest, hottest, or coldest of things. Some of the valleys just back of the northern and southern coastal strips are rich in scenery and livability and do not lay claim to the superlatives that accompany many of California's features.

Explore California through the written word. Immerse yourself in the photographic imagery of the poetic beauty and go for a vicarious vacation *Discovering California* for yourself.

Northern Mountains

Like a rumpled blanket, the northern part of California is clothed in complicated mountain systems, with minor interruptions from coast to eastern border. In the northwest the different mountain structures are grouped for convenience under the heading of Klamath Mountains, although their various natures would seem to preclude much relationship except for their occurrence in the same area. The so-called Klamath Mountains merge into the Coast Range on the west and to the east they merge with the southern Cascades. The Warner Mountains in the northeast are a separate block of fault-scarp ridges that rise like a mini-Sierra above a high plain, in what is probably the least known and least visited part of California's northern environs.

If the eastern corner is remote and unknown, the whole interior north portion of the state follows that pattern to a slightly lesser degree. Lack of roads and the rugged nature of the terrain have enabled the extreme north to remain isolated in an era when isolation on the planet seems to be a major achievement. Considering further that the area is a part of the most populous state, the situation is indeed an anomaly. But because it is such a *physical* landscape, it has successfully resisted large-scale incursion or alteration by man.

Take the northwest behind the coastal mountains. The major distinct ranges are the Siskiyou, Marble, Trinity, Salmon and Scott Mountain systems. Together they comprise a wilderness kingdom as wild as any in California and far less frequented than the mountain barrier that is California's trademark — the Sierra Nevada.

For all their ruggedness, the mountains of the northwest welcome the explorer. The hiker and the back-road traveler have no difficulty reaching this particular Shangri-La, even if it is in high country. An example would be the Trinity Alps, the glaciated peaks of the Trinity Range, rising parallel to the north south Trinity River. Thompson Peak, the highest in the group at 9,000 feet, shoulders a heavy glacial load. The Trinities have been compared to the Sierras in the brusque thrust of the granite peaks, but they are closer knit, so trails into them are shorter. They differ from the Sierras in another noteworthy particular. Their relative nearness to the coast gives them more precipitation than the bigger range down south. So their streams are more frequent and the vegetation is generally dense and very lush. Their attractiveness is enhanced by the warmth of the canyons and by the moisture-cooled heights.

The Salmon-Trinity Alps are designated a wilderness area. So have the Marble Mountains north of them. The Marbles are rugged too, but their configuration is different. Their name is traceable to the limestone and marble streaking evident in some of the more monumental landmarks of the range. These mountains are not quite as lofty as the Trinities, but they are no less an adventure for the outdoor explorer. They are well laced with scenic trails used by hikers and horseback riders. Packing into the area on horseback is the preferred way to visit the interior of this wilderness, since the four-legged species is better adept for carrying supplies than the two-legged backpacker. The various trails lead to small high elevation lakes — about 50 of them — that are crystal pure and complete with trout. On the way to the lakes, there is a thick fragrant forest of pine, hemlock, fir and spruce trees. The dozen or more cold water streams found in this wilderness are good fishing waters, too. For people who are satisfied with observing, there are plenty of land based residents of these mountains who roam about dressed in nothing but fur. To sight them it takes a little stealth

10

on the part of a visitor, be he on foot or horseback. But caution and perseverance will eventually pay off, and one may possibly trade stares with a bear, deer, or even a mountain lion. What makes this easy on latter-day animal trackers is the system of campgrounds maintained by the Forest Service in various section of the Marble Mountain Wilderness.

The Klamath River is the big waterway in these parts. It is paralleled by State Highway 96, as the river's canyon is the only low-level passageway through all of these mountains. The river comes into California about midway on the border with Oregon and winds south and west through the northwest mountains falling to the coast. Being the centerpiece, so to speak, of these wild mountains, it is a good starting point from tourist towns like Happy Camp to launch trips into the interior.

The northern mountains had their version of the Gold Rush, when California was the *Valhalla* of the hordes who sought the yellow metal. The Sierra foothills were the main arenas, but the frantic activity at those foothills had a smaller-scale parallel in the north. There are still testimonials to that sometimes rough-and-tumble era of the mid-1800s. The town of Weaverville, just south of the Salmon-Trinity Alps Wilderness on the Trinity River, is one of these survivors of the early days. Shasta is another. They still have relics that remind us of their beginning — buildings, mines, wide streets (for turning horse-drawn wagons), and so on. The famed Joss House in Weaverville is preserved as a state historic park and is reminiscent of the time when the population of the town included 3,000 Chinese.

Shasta Valley and the Sacramento Gorge define the boundary between the mountains of the northwest. The southern Cascades push into California on the eastern side of the two valleys. The Cascades set their mark on California with the biggest, best known mountain in the northern part of the state. Visible for 100-miles around, Mt. Shasta ranks sixth for height (14,162 feet) in the hierarchy of California peaks. Undeniably first for sheer impressiveness and drama, Mount Shasta is a symmetrical volcanic cone that still carries five glaciers on its higher elevations. The wide-based white giant rises majestically out of an apron of forested lower slopes. The enchantment in its aspect is especially powerful in the early morning and late afternoon, when the orange-pink light may paint its summit in a shimmering brilliance. In times like these, Shasta seems the ultimate expression of nature's skill at pulling off the grand gesture.

Shasta must share some of its glory with a satellite cone, Shastina, lower down on the western slope. Their volcanic personality is demonstrated not only in their shape but in the wisps of vapor that still issue from high crevices, as if the mountains are getting up steam for some future orgy of fire and ashes. In this century the shining twin peaks of Shasta and Shastina have been upstaged somewhat by another big volcanic peak, about 40-miles southeast of Redding at the southern end of the Cascades. Mount Lassen, the centerpiece of a ridge of cinder cones in Lassen Volcanic National Park, actually erupted through 1914 to 1917, throwing rocks and spewing hot lava over surrounding valleys. Some of the cones in this area are very young, having been born within the past 500 years. An example is the Chaos Crags, a weird jumble of sharply angled rocks that sprang from Lassen's base on the northwest.

Lassen is obviously a region of young volcanics. The evidence is still very fresh from Lassen's recent activity as the lava looks *new* and the trees that were killed by thermal activity litter the terrain. The heart of the Lassen country is open only by trail, but the entire park is within a day's hiking distance of a road. The Lassen Peak Road goes around a portion of the National Park and anyone traveling this passage is able to see a wide panorama of the effects of volcanism on the land. The high road opens up an extraordinary vista reaching far beyond the confines of the park. On all sides there are grand natural structures in the distance. Mt. Shasta on the northwest, the Sierra to the south, and the jumble of mountains on the west are all aspects of the extravagant scenery that encircles this strange volcanic disarray.

The Warner Mountains and Valley of the northeast corner have traditionally been isolated from the California mainstream, partly because of their distance from everything else. This corner of the state has some unusual geology, such as high alluvial plains of unusual flatness, yet frequent mountains and generally stony soils. With the exceptions of the deserts, this is the state's most thinly populated region. Ranching is the primary activity of the residents, with use of range closely supervised by the federal government through its control of national forest lands. The Warner Range is a corrugated fault-scarp assemblage of alpine mountains quite as impressive, on a smaller scale, as the Sierras. The Warner Mountains rise gradually on the western side, but their eastern face is steep and abrupt. The loftier southern heights are included in the South Warner Wilderness, where solitude can be as complete as California or any other place can offer. The South Warner Wilderness can be explored by hiking a 24-mile trail that lies partly along the summit ridge then drops into rocky lowlands and meadows of wildflowers. Some side trails lead to dales and creeks where the trout fishing is good, according to the few fishermen who try their luck in these alpine fortresses.

The recreational potential of the remote northeast is still unrealized, but that is probably the most important reason for its attractiveness to the relatively few vacationers who have found it. The lake and mountain areas are refuges not only for people but for the bird and animal species who also prefer the less glittery parts of the Golden State. In addition to the waters of the Warner Range, the northeast has a large number of lakes. The best known of the lakes is probably Tule Lake, a national wildlife refuge, located in the western region of northeast California near the border with Oregon. This 30,000-acre preserve is a crucial stop for wildfowl on the Pacific flyway. Down in a southeast direction near Susanville, the big city of the northeast, is a human-life refuge, Eagle Lake. The long, narrow lake is one of California's bigger bodies of fresh water and it is becoming a popular recreation area.

Sierra Nevada

To begin on a proper note, the Sierra is the biggest unified mountain range in the continental United States. The long mountain barrier covers a large portion of eastern California, hunching its shoulders over fertile valleys on the west and withered desert land on the east. One of the lofty points on its crest, Mt. Whitney reaching an elevation of 14,494 feet, was long the tallest mountain in the United States until Alaska's Mt. McKinley, located in Denali National Park, was admitted to the Union. But tall is definitely not *all* when the Sierra is concerned. Nature seems to have gone to extraordinary lengths to do something original when she built this giant fault block.

The western foothills of the range reach into the Sacramento and San Joaquin valleys. Rising a step south of Lassen Volcanic National Park, the Sierra Nevada Mountains add 4,000 miles of steep and spiny granite wall to the California scene. They reach south to Tejon Pass where the Tehachapi Mountains near Los Angeles close it off. The range is about 70-miles wide through much of its length and covers 27,000-square miles. That is extensive coverage. But mere statistics do not begin to tell the story of the Sierras, either in space or in time. Anybody who knows something about them is usually aware that there is more to learn.

Like that vast mountain chain to the east, the Rocky Mountains, the present version of the Sierras is not the first version, geologists have determined. A so-called Ancestral Sierra, not as high as the current range, emerged some time back in the hazy geological past and eventually was worn down over millions of years. This ancient Sierra was composed not only of sedimentary rock but it had a molten base that eventually cooled to form a lighter-hued granitic rock. With the raising of the present range, the base rock was pushed up to form the major part of the Sierra's mass. This light colored bedrock, brought into relief by the massive sculpturing job performed over the eons by the glaciers of the Ice Age and by water erosion, is the primary ingredient in the dazzling spectacle that characterizes the Sierra all along its southerly portion.

The Sierra is generally lower in the north and higher in the south. Although it is called a unified range, it is far from an uncomplicated one. Glaciers have carved fissures, canyons and valleys into its uplifted mass. Fault lines have produced colossal cliff structures such as those in Yosemite Valley. The volcanism that contributed to the Sierra's birth is still not entirely unnoticed. The sedimentary rocks that formed part of the ancestral range can be found on the lower western foothills. Powerful streams dash along its gullies, feeding the watercourses of the Central Valley. Some of California's major rivers originate on its western slopes: the Feather, Yuba, and Bear in the north, and the Tuolumne, Merced, and San Joaquin rivers farther south.

It was April, 1776, when Franciscan Fray Pedro Font first gazed eastward from Antioch upon the massive mountain range that is now known as the backbone of California. So inspired by what he viewed, he expressed, "If we looked to the east we saw on the other side of the plain at a distance of some thirty leagues a great Sierra Nevada, white from the summit to the skirts, and running diagonally almost from south-southeast to north-northeast." The Spanish words *Sierra Nevada* translate to mean "snowy mountain range." Indeed, it is a mountain world that stretches through more than five degrees of latitude and reaches elevations of more than 14,000 feet, likely to have a variety of climates. This is generally true of the Sierra Nevada, although its general precipitation regime is in line with the state's pattern of much less moisture in summer than in winter. The northern range gets the most moisture. Donner Summit, the route of the only freeway over the range (Interstate Highway 80) is the center of a High Sierra region that gets an average annual snowfall of 400 inches. Temperatures vary, obviously, from north to south and with variations in altitude. For example the lower western slopes of the north share the warm summers of the Sacramento Valley. Higher elevations have cooler summers. The crests sometimes get extremely cold, even in summer. The Sierra foothills that border the southerly San Joaquin Valley are hot and dry like the basin is in the summer, but things cool off as the altitude increases. Winters in the southern Sierra are cold but usually not severe, except at the highest altitudes. The northern part is a different story, as the tragedy-ridden Donner party discovered in 1846 when they tried to breach the 7,239-foot pass in the winter.

The modern millions of Californians think of the Sierra as a playground and vacationland rather than a fierce mountain wall. They have made its landmark features some of the most popular travel destinations in the country. The human feeling of affinity with the Sierra may have begun with the wild days of the Gold Rush, when thousands of would-be instant millionaires concentrated in the western foothills of the range. Possibly, in between digging gold out of the rocks and scooping it from the streams, some of them did some looking around and forgot their prospecting for a while in the awesome presence of their surroundings. Whatever their reaction to the mountains, some of their towns, or remnants of them, still live in the northern foothill country of the Feather River Canyon. These relics draw present-day travelers to the Sierra precincts, and inevitably some of them go on to explore the fascinating interior of the range that has nothing to do with gold and mines.

The best remembered of the gold camps, which became a town in that region, is Oroville. It still sits where the Feather River comes down out of the Sierra foothills. And it is still not much bigger than it was when it ran entirely on dreams of gold. Many of the residents during the early days were Chinese, among the large numbers of Orientals who came to California during the 19-century to build the railroads and work in the mines. Oroville's Chinese Temple still exists,

California Poppy (*Eschscholzia californica*)**, Antelope Valley California Poppy Reserve**

The official state flower for California is the golden poppy, chosen in 1903 from a group of three flowers, the golden poppy, the white poppy, and the Mariposa lily. As one of the earliest blooming wildflowers in California, the rolling hills near Lancaster in southern California, north of Los Angeles, shimmer in a blaze of glowing gold. West of Lancaster and south of the Tehachapi Mountains is an area "established to protect and perpetuate outstanding displays of native wildflowers, particularly the California Poppy…." As part of the Mojave State Parks, the 1,745- acre Antelope Valley California Poppy Reserve becomes a palette of color when wildflowers are at their best, which occurs from March through May. Mid-April is usually the peak viewing time. *Photography by James Blank*

Laguna Beach along the Pacific Ocean

The rising San Joaquin Hills, reaching heights over 900 feet, provide a backdrop to the Pacific Ocean coastline of southern California above the city of Laguna Beach. Crystal Cove State Park is just north of Laguna Beach, providing over three-miles of secluded coastline and "2,000 acres of undeveloped woodland," a stark contrast from the heavily invaded San Joaquin Hills and Pacific coastline seen here. The large beach near Reef Point is the "fun center" for sunbathers and swimmers, and for beach games. Pelican Point is a more reserved area where picnicking and surf fishing are the favorite sports. The State Park extends beyond the coastline out into the Pacific where skin divers and scuba divers enjoy the underwater-exploration areas protected by the park.

Photography by James Blank

Mount Shasta, Cascade Mountain Range, Northern California

Visible for one-hundred-miles around, Mount Shasta ranks sixth for height (14,162 feet) in the hierarchy of California peaks. It is undeniably first for sheer impressiveness and drama. Mount Shasta is a symmetrical volcanic cone that still carries five glaciers on its higher elevations. The wide-based white giant rises majestically out of an apron of forested lower slopes in the Shasta-Trinity National Forest. The enchantment in its aspect is especially powerful in the early morning and late afternoon, when the light paints its summit in a shimmering brilliance. Shasta must share some of its glory with a satellite cone titled Shastina.

Photography by Shangle Photographics

Shasta Dam and Lake Shasta, Southern Cascade Mountains, Northern California

According to the Bureau of Reclamation, the Department of the Interior, "Shasta Dam is a curved concrete gravity structure with an embankment wing dam….Shasta Dam serves to control floodwaters and store surplus water runoff for irrigation in the Sacramento and San Joaquin Valleys, along with providing maintenance of navigation flows and conservation of fish in the Sacramento River [and for the protection of the] Sacramento-San Joaquin Delta from intrusion of saline ocean water, [and] provides water for industrial use, and generates hydroelectric electricity… The powerplant is located to the right of the spillway and has five main generating units supplied by 15-foot-diameter penstocks." The water drainage area for the reservoir encompasses 6,665-square-miles. It was a six-year-project for the completion of Shasta Dam, beginning in 1938, with modification in 1995 and 1996. The structural height of the dam is 602 feet, holding water that creates Shasta Lake. Twelve-miles-south of Shasta Dam on Interstate Highway 5 is the city of Redding.

Photography by James Blank

Giant Sequoia Redwoods in Sequoia National Forest, Sierra Nevada Mountains

As stated by the American Museum of Natural History, "the only sequoia species left are the giant sequoia of the Sierra Nevada in central California…." The National Park Service states that "…The largest of the sequoias are as tall as an average 26-story building, and their diameters at the base exceed the width of many city streets. As they continue to grow, they produce about 40 cubic feet of wood each year, approximately equal to the volume of a 50-foot-tall tree one-foot in diameter. The largest sequoia is titled General Sherman, exceeding a height of 275 feet with a circumference beyond 102 feet. The third largest tree, the General Grant, attains over 267 feet and is honored with the title of the Nation's Christmas Tree, receiving the honor from President Coolidge in 1926. President Dwight Eisenhower bestowed the honor of National Shrine to the tree in 1956.

Photography by James Blank

Hearst Castle™, San Simeon, South-central Pacific Coast

William Randolph Hearst left a legacy that is difficult to match. At age 23 Mr. Hearst proved to his family and peers that he was "capable" of running a newspaper, and that command of the business led to a one-time ownership of over twenty-four newspapers. His achievements in the business world have him identified with the newspaper and magazine industry, as well as the movie industry, radio and television. In 1922 Mr. Hearst began the construction of a dream home that he referred to as *La Cuesta Encantada*™ (the Enchanted Hills™) in the Santa Lucia Mountains at an elevation of some 1,600 feet. Full-time occupancy was achieved in 1927. The view of the Pacific Ocean and San Simeon Bay is unequalled. Mr. Hearst lived to the age of 88. He died in August, 1951.

Photography by Shangle Photographics

Dana Point Harbor, Dana Point, Southern Pacific Coastline

One of Orange County's favorite places is Dana Point, about halfway between Los Angeles and San Diego on the Pacific Ocean. A favorite of boaters Dana Point Harbor is a casting-off point for excursions to Catalina Island and for annual Grey Whale excursions from December through March, and for launching a sport-fishing trip. The annual Tallships Festival is held in September on Labor Day Weekend. Historic Tallships and Great Schooners gather off Dana Point and make a grand entrance into the harbor, providing a spectacular display. Orange County Marine Institute provides educational adventures with "educational programs for children and adults including a lecture series as well as other types of specialty educational cruises."

Photography by James Blank

Anza-Borrego Desert State Park®, Colorado Desert

No one can say it better than Anza-Borrego Desert State Park®. "With over 600,000 acres, Anza-Borrego Desert State Park® is the largest desert State Park in the contiguous United States. [Five–hundred] miles of dirt roads, two huge wilderness areas (comprising 2/3 of the park) and 110-miles of riding and hiking trails provide visitors with an unparalleled opportunity to experience the wonders of the Colorado Desert. The park name is derived from a combination of the name of Spanish explorer Juan Bautista de Anza and the Spanish word *borrego*," referring to bighorn sheep. The park features washes, wildflowers, palm groves, cacti and sweeping vistas. Visitors may also have the chance to see roadrunners, golden eagles, kit foxes, mule deer and bighorn sheep as well as desert iguanas, chuckwallas and four species of rattlesnake." The city of Borrego Springs services the residential needs and is often listed as the hottest place in the United States during the summer season.

Photography by Shangle Photographics

Ubehebe Crater, Death Valley National Park

The size of this crater extends about one-half-mile in width and to nearly 800 feet in depth. Violent volcanic steam explosions created this huge hole over 6,000 years ago. Hiking trails lead down to the floor of the crater and a rim trail allows a 1.5-mile excursion walk. The severe bleakness of the area is displayed in the withered appearance reflected in the austere rock formations.

Photography by James Blank

Emerald Bay in Lake Tahoe, Sierra Nevada Mountains, eastern California

Crystal-blue water of Lake Tahoe creates Emerald Bay, located on the southern tip of the lake in Eldorado National Forest. Lake Tahoe measures 22-miles long, north-to-south, and 12-miles wide, east-to-west. The surface altitude is 6,229 feet and the maximum depth is 1,650 feet. "California's first underwater shipwreck park, Emerald Bay Historic Barges, was officially opened to the public" in 1994, allowing underwater explorations of historic vintage barges that sank in the cold, clear water.

Photography by Shangle Photographic

Morro Bay Harbor and Morro Rock, South-central Pacific Coastline

The city of Morro Bay took its name from the famous monolith landmark, Morro Rock, named by Portuguese explorer Juan Rodriguez Cabrillo during his 16th-century explorations of the California coastline. Morro Rock rises 578 feet out of the Pacific Ocean, sheltering the small fishing village and harbor, each named Morro Bay. Migratory birds find winter haven at Morro Bay, an actual seabird rookery. The annual Morro Bay Winter Bird Festival "is celebrated each year … over the Martin Luther King Birthday Weekend. … [The area] is a Globally Important Bird Area on the Pacific Flyway." The Morro Bay State Park Museum of Natural History is equipped with "state of the art video display and interactive exhibit." Morro Bay is a stepping stone to many well equipped cultural information centers and to excellent camping facilities, such as Morro Bay State Park, Morro Strand State Beach and Morro Rock Natural Preserve.

Photography by Shangle Photographics

Point Bonita Lighthouse, Marin Peninsula, entrance to San Francisco Bay

The rolling waves of the Pacific Ocean pound against the foundation rocks of Point Bonita Lighthouse, built at this site in 1877. The first lighthouse, lighted in 1855, was located on the highest hill in the area, but the thick fog that often shrouded the lighthouse negated the effect of the light. A cannon was brought to the site and was fired as a fog signal, a rather constant noise since fog was so ever present. The lighthouse was relocated to the farthest point on Marin Peninsula, allowing for a more easily seen beacon. A hiking trail works its way to the lighthouse along a one-and-one-half-mile trail. The Coast Guard maintains the light, but as part of the Golden Gate National Recreational Area, the Park Service maintains the historic contact for visitors.

Photography by Shangle Photographics

Mission San Carlos Borroméo de Carmelo, Carmel-by-the-Sea

Named for the 16th-century cardinal, St. Charles of Borroméo, Mission Carmel, as known by many, was established on June 3, 1770, on the shore of Monterey Bay by the Spanish Franciscan padre, Fray Junipero Serra. He arrived by ship, the *San Antonio,* from San Diego and met the overland group led by Don Gaspar de Portola who left San Diego in mid-May. The presidio that housed Spanish soldiers and the new mission remained side by side for just a year. The mission was moved to its current site, south to the Carmel Valley along the Carmel River. The move protected the Native Americans from the badgering soldiers. Mission San Carlos Borroméo de Carmelo was the second mission of the twenty-one missions established in California. *Photography by Robert D. Shangle*

South Fork of the Kings River, Kings Canyon/Sequoia National Park

This rapidly flowing stream gives a false impression regarding its true nature. Referred to by experienced river runners, this wild and scenic river is "one of California's last untamed and unspoiled wilderness waterways." April is the most spectacular time for whitewater river rafting, with water reaching its most abundant flow during the months of May and June. The scenic greenery changes with the seasons, beginning as soft lush foliage, spattered with colors from spring wildflowers. Fun for the entire family is what is reported about the waters of the South Fork of the Kings River. Rapids are rated Class III, III+ and IV for difficulty.

Photography by Shangle Photographics

The Lone Cypress at Pebble Beach, Monterey Peninsula on the Pacific Ocean

Anchored into the granite headland of Monterey Peninsula, the small cypress tree known reverently as the Lone Cypress is one of California's most famous landmarks. This tree beckons photographer and artist. The famous 17-Mile Drive around the peninsula affords many landmark sites. Spanish Bay holds the history of Spanish exploration and settlement of California's second mission, Mission San Carlos Borroméo de Carmelo. There is Point Joe, where turbulent waters froth and spew, and Bird Rock and Seal Rock, well known rookeries. Crocker Grove is a naturally grown 13-acre stand of ancient Monterey Cypress that grows exclusively on the Monterey Peninsula and at Point Lobos State Preserve, south of Carmel. The road winds through the Grove past the Lone Cypress and the "Ghost Tree", Pescadero Point and along Stillwater Cove Beach and Pebble Beach Golf Links. The southern exit of the Drive leads to the town of Carmel-by-the-Sea. The northern entrance of the Drive is near the restful town of Pacific Grove, home of the Monarch Grove Sanctuary, so well known for the Monarch Butterfly. The eastern approach is from Monterey, an exciting coastal marine city with an abundance of history.

Photography by Shangle Photographics

The RMS Queen Mary in the city of Long Beach

Self-boasting is the best way to appreciate what the *Queen Mary* has to offer. "A floating city awash in elegance, the *Queen Mary*, listed on the National Register of Historic Places, remains one of the most famous ships in history." The keel was laid in December, 1930, and the first launch happened on September 26, 1934. Her maiden voyage was a five-day trip to New York City departing from Southampton May 27, 1936. During World War II the *Queen Mary* became a troopship, starting in 1940. Her final troop-carrying voyage was to New York, arriving April 4, 1945. After renovation in 1946, the *Queen Mary* returned to her luxury greatness, carrying passengers until retirement in 1967, with a total of 1,001 crossings of the Atlantic to her crossing card. As a luxury hotel with multiple amenities and attractions, the *Queen Mary* is berthed at the mouth of Queensway Bay. The city of Long Beach, founded in the late 19th century as a resort town, has grown from three-square-miles in size with 1,500 residents in 1897 to California's fifth-largest city, encompassing some 50-square-miles and a general census of some 500,000 people. Oil was discovered in 1921 on Signal Hill and again in 1936, establishing an economic soundness to the area. Long known as a Navy town, the U.S. Naval base was constructed in the harbor in 1941. The city of Long Beach states that "it offers a unique combination of strategic location, excellent climate, shoreline beauty, and Southern California lifestyle, wrapped up in one package. From the emphasis on the "three T's" (Trade, Tourism and Technology), to the city's bountiful array of business and residential neighborhoods, it's no wonder Long Beach is quickly becoming one of the leading regions for business, tourism and community in the west."

Photography by James Blank

Yosemite Falls, Yosemite National Park, Sierra Nevada Mountain Range

Magnificent Yosemite Falls drops 1,430 feet to a cascading basin of the Merced River that continues out to the Lower Falls that drops 320 feet. With the multiple tumbling cascades between the two waterfalls, an overall drop of 2,425 feet is achieved, creating one of the world's highest waterfall units. Just one of the wonders found in Yosemite National Park, Yosemite Falls finds its equal-of-importance with the massive sheer rock walls and huge rock domes, the largest being El Capitan, "a granite buttress that rises 3,604 feet from the valley floor." *Photography by James Blank*

Bodie, the ghost town in the Sierra Nevada Range, East-central California

Waterman S. Body (or Bodey) discovered gold in 1859. By 1877 Bodie (the name spelling was recorded with authorities to insure the correct pronunciation) was a *high flying town* that lasted through 1881, inhabited by about 10,000 people and consisted of about 2,000 buildings that included sixty saloons and dance halls and seven breweries that operated 24-hours a day. It was *the* mining town, supported by one of the richest gold discoveries in the West, producing more than 32-million-dollars of gold and 6 - to 7-million [dollars]in silver." Records indicate that would-be, get-rich-quick miners flocked to the area bringing some of the most wicked, wildest and lawless attitudes found anywhere. Mine production reached its peak in 1882 when serious downturns occurred, many mines went out bankrupt. A serious fire in 1892 destroyed many buildings. In 1932 a major fire destroyed 90 percent of what remained of this once bustling community. Today the "Ghost Town" of Bodie is registered as a National Historic Site and a State Historic Park. Bodie is located south of Bridgeport in Mono County, east of U.S. Highway 395 on State Road 270 near the Nevada border, north of Mono Lake.

Photography by James Blank

Mount Lassen and Manzanita Lake, Lassen National Volcanic Park, Northern California

Mount Lassen is the centerpiece of a ridge of cinder cones in Lassen Volcanic National Park, which actually erupted through 1914 to 1917, throwing rocks and spewing hot lava over the surrounding valley. Some of the cones in this area are very young, having been born within the past 500 years. The heart of the Lassen country is open only by trail, but the entire park is within a day's hiking distance of a road. The high road opens up an extraordinary vista reaching far beyond the confines of the park: Mount Shasta on the northwest, the Sierra to the south, and the jumble of mountains on the west.

Photography by James Blank

Golden Gate Bridge at San Francisco

Begun as a topic of conversation in 1872, the massive suspension bridge named the Golden Gate became a reality to pedestrian traffic on May 27, 1937 and to vehicular traffic on the following day, May 28th spanning the San Francisco Bay from Marin County to the city of San Francisco. For a bridge some insisted could not be constructed and for those who stated the cost would be $100-million-dollars, the bridge became a reality with a cost of about $73-million-dollars, which included $39-million in interest on the principal bond that was retired in 1971. All monies used for bond payment were received from bridge tolls. The over-all length of the bridge is 1.7 miles, or 8,981 feet. The color of the Golden Gate Bridge is known as "International Orange," painted with orange vermilion paint. For your next game of "do-you-know?" the Golden Gate Research Library states there are approximately 600,000 rivets in each tower on the bridge. The city referred to by many people as the *jewel of the north coast* is San Francisco, one of the few really great cities in the world. Its magic comes from many elements, among them its air conditioned weather, tolerant philosophy, up-and-down streets, fascinating architecture, and land-sea ambience.

Photography by James Blank

Mount Whitney, Sierra Nevada Mountains, East-central California

The highest point in the contiguous 48-states is Mount Whitney, reaching a height of 14,495 feet above sea level. This craggy peak is surrounded by equally massive mountains: Florence Peak at 12,405 feet, Alta Peak at 11, 204 feet, Barton Peak at 10, 350 feet, Palmer Mountain at 11,250 feet, and Olancho Peak at 12,123 feet. To view Mount Whitney is quite difficult as these neighbors tower at such heights that it is difficult to obtain an open site. This grouping of mountains is located within Sequoia and Kings Canyon National Parks, not far from the Giant Forest of giant sequoia trees. This is a hiker's paradise with 800 miles of trails. Lodging and camping facilities are available at specific locations within the parks.

Photography by Shangle Photographics

Autumn in the Sierra Nevada Mountain Range near Big Pine, Eastern California

Big Pine is a small town south of Bishop on U.S. Highway 395 where the Owens River flows. West of Big Pine are wilderness-hiking trails in the high Sierra Nevada Mountains, particularly in the largest glacier in the Sierra, Palisade Glacier, rising some 14,000 feet above sea level and in Big Pine Canyon. Numerous lakes are scattered throughout this high country, where there is good fishing for Rainbow, Golden and Brook trout. North of Big Pine is the Ancient Bristlecone Pine Forest, located in the White Mountains in the Inyo National Forest. The Bristlecone Pine is the oldest living tree on earth, exceeding the age of the Giant Sequoia by over a thousand years.

Photography by James Blank

Near Garberville, Humboldt County, Northwest California

One might believe the word *paradise* is the name for this lovely area in northwest California. There are so many things to see here. Humboldt Redwoods State Park is a 51,000-acre forest just off U.S. Highway 101 that allows a tremendous viewing of the Avenue of Giants, massive redwood trees. Beautiful clear flowing rivers such as the Eel and Mattole provide excellent opportunites for fishing and swimming. There are camping facilities and fine lodging sites. Hiking trails allow a deeper penetration of the pristine area. Travel farther north along U.S. Highway 101 to Eureka and visit Humboldt State Historic Park. Continue on to Redwood National Park to see beautiful Coast Redwood groves, then on to Del Norte Redwoods State Park and to Jedediah Smith Redwoods State Park. Both parks are within the Redwood National Park. *Photography by Shangle Photographics*

Rocky coastline of the Pacific Ocean south of Carmel-by-the-Sea along the Big Sur

Some of the most beautiful ocean shoreline in America is right here. The Big Sur, a section of California's most scenic coastline, is defined as extending from the Carmel River State Beach south to San Simeon State Park along State Highway 1. Several State Parks, rich in camping facilities, are along the route and they provide excellent interpretive centers and opportunities to explore the shoreline for sea creatures and inland to areas of great interest. The Ventana Wilderness Society "has joined together with the Big Sur Historical Society and the California Department of Parks and Recreation to create an interpretive center in Andrew Molera State Park" known as the Ventana Wilderness Society Research and Education Center. Through efforts of the Society the California Condor and the bald eagle have been reintroduced to the area. Their purpose is "to perpetuate plant and animal species native to the central coast of California through wildlife and habitat restoration, research and education." *Photography by Shangle Photographics*

The city of Newport Beach, Southern California

California State Highway 1 skirts the Pacific Ocean moving through many heavily populated areas, including Newport Beach, comprising the communities of Balboa, Balboa Island, Bay Shores, Corona del Mar, Harbor Island, Lido Isle, Linda Isle and Newport Heights. Boating opportunities are far reaching from Newport Bay, home to one of the largest yachting and boating centers in the United States. A six-mile-long-sandy peninsula protects the communities and harbor from the turbulent waters of the Pacific Ocean.

Photography by James Blank

Point Arena Lighthouse, Mendocino County

The Point Arena Lighthouse began operating in 1870. Severally damaged during the 1906 earthquake that caused devastation to San Francisco, the lighthouse was reconstructed of steel-reinforced concrete and re-lighted in 1908. The tower height is 115 feet. Located along Mendocino County's windy Pacific Ocean shoreline, the small town of Point Arena is two-miles-south of the lighthouse on State Highway 1 and the artistic town of Mendocino is thirty-miles-north. Manchester State Park is immediately north of the lighthouse. *Photography by Shangle Photographics*

Alcatraz Island in San Francisco Bay

Custodial care of Alcatraz is under the jurisdiction of the National Park Service who best explains Alcatraz. "Out in the middle of the San Francisco Bay, the island of Alcatraz is a world unto itself. Isolation, one of the constants of island life for any inhabitant — soldier, guard, prisoner, bird or plant — is a recurrent theme in the unfolding history of Alcatraz. Alcatraz Island is one of Golden Gate National Recreation Area's most popular destinations, offering a close-up look at a historic and infamous federal prison long off-limits to the public. Visitors to the island can not only explore the remnants of the prison, but learn about the Native American occupation of 1969 – 1971, early military fortifications and the West Coast's first (and oldest operating) lighthouse. These structures and the island's many natural features — gardens, tide pools, bird colonies, and bay views beyond compare, are being preserved by the National Park Service which is working to make it accessible to visitors, preserve its buildings, protect its birds and other wildlife, and interpret its history."

Photography by Robert Shangle

City of Santa Barbara along the Pacific Ocean shoreline, Santa Barbara County

The city of Santa Barbara gets a head start in the *beautiful-city* sweepstakes by reason of its location. Its setting and climate are often compared to those of the Mediterranean of European stature. The Santa Ynes Mountains reach down to the coast and enfold the city in a natural amphitheater, culminating in a small crescent bay. Santa Barbara's leisurely style of life seems appropriate in such a setting and with such a gentle climate. High above the valley and waters of the Pacific Ocean, Mission Santa Barbara, "Queen of the Missions", was founded on December 4, 1786. The first church was built in 1789, a second church was completed five years later and destroyed by an earthquake in 1812, leading to the construction of the church recognized today. *Photography by James Blank*

Burney Falls, McArthur-Burney Falls Memorial State Park, Northeast California

Located in the northeast section of the Shasta-Trinity National Forest is beautiful Burney Falls, cascading 129 feet into a clear, shimmering pool. The porous volcanic basalt rock releases the captured water accumulated during rain and snow weather, creating the magnificent waterfall. McArthur-Burney Falls Memorial State Park is home to the waterfall, named for pioneer settler, Samuel Burney, who occupied the area in the 1850s. *Photography by James Blank*

State Capitol, Sacramento

Following designs of the United States Capitol, California is favored with a handsome building created of marble granite, completed in 1874. The building was subjected to a major reconstruction during the 1970s following concerns by lawmakers regarding the sureness of the building during any potential earthquake episode. California history is an integral part of the Capitol, where the Capitol Museum is housed within the Capitol and managed by the California Department of Parks and Recreation. The city of Sacramento was founded in 1849 and soon became the gateway to gold country.

Photography by James Blank

Pacific Ocean shoreline at Mendocino, Mendocino County

Northern California has a special place saved for those who enjoy a relaxing lifestyle and the natural beauty Mother Nature provides in abundance. The city of Mendocino releases the serenity of the coastal atmosphere captured by artisians. The charm of the rocky shores, the historical treasures and the old New England architecture beckon travelers to linger. Russian Gulch State Park is nearby providing about one-and-one-half miles of ocean frontage that provides dazzling sunsets. The Mendocino Coast Botanical Garden is here, comprised of 47 acres of exquisite gardens of great variety, specializing in Rhododendrons, Camilllias, Pacifica Iris, Fern, Heather, Heritage Roses, Fern gardens, and many more items growing in the garden. The mission of the Garden "is to display, interpret, and nurture our unique gardens and the ecology of the Mendocino Coast." *Photography by Shangle Photographics*

City of San Diego and Shelter Harbor

Silver Strand State Beach is located between the Pacific Ocean and San Diego Bay and between Imperial Beach on the south and the city of Coronado on the north. It goes without saying that San Diego is ideal for sailing enthusiasts. It was an enthusiastic Portugese sailor Juan Rodríguez Cabrillo who first sited and entered San Diego Bay in 1542. To-day, Cabrillo National Monument located at Point Loma honors the European explorer. There are many anchorage sites for sailors as well as launching areas. San Diego is home to the famous 1,400-acre Balboa Park that offers a phenomenal amount of history with exceptional museums and gardens. North of the city is famous Mission Bay and Pacific Beach. San Diego began as the first Mission in California in 1769, established by Fray Junipero Serra, and was the first permanent Spanish settlement in California. When restoration began on the mission building, only the façade of the church and the base of the belfry were in evidence. The beautiful garden in Mission San Diego de Alcala provides a center for solitude, reflection and a glimpse into mission history. *Photography by James Blank*

The beautiful Pacific Ocean shoreline of Big Sur, Southern California

California has more than 1,000 miles of Pacific Ocean frontage in a number of guises, all of them gorgeous. In the north the coastal visage is rugged and dramatic. The smooth, sunny and populous beaches to the south have become symbols of an entire lifestyle. In between the California coast can equal or exceed the phenomena of any other state's coastline.

Photography by Shangle Photographics

Fields of crops in the Salinas Valley near Soledad, West-central California

If it grows in the ground, California probably produces it. If it grows on a tree, California probably produces it. These fields display as an artist pallet displays hues of green, but add drops of red and it could be fields of tomatoes, with the help of the imagination. Fruits, vegetables, and nuts are high producing crops in California along with cotton, wheat and rice. According to the California Department of Food and Agriculture, records support production of "42% of all U.S. fruit & nuts… " as well as "55% of all U.S. vegetables." Statistics vary from year to year. "For more than 50 consecutive years, California has been the number one food and agricultural producer in the United States." And of interest, 20% of what California grows is exported.

Photography by Robert Shangle

Monterey Bay, Pacific Ocean

Gaze over the rocky outcrop and view the vast expanse of Monterey Bay, that picturesque section of Pacific Ocean water that laps the shoreline to the north of Monterey Peninsula. Point Pinos Lighthouse, located on the northernmost tip of the Monterey Peninsula, guards the southern entrance to the Bay and has been active since 1855, making it the oldest continuously operating lighthouse on the Pacific Ocean coast. Excellent state-beach parks, eleven in total, edge the bay's shoreline beginning at Monterey State Beach and culminating at Natural Bridges State Beach at Santa Cruz. The cities of Pacific Grove and Monterey are located on the southern portion of the Bay, tucked next to Monterey Peninsula. Seaside, Marina, Castroville, Watsonville, Aptos, and Capitola are located throughout the semi-circular drive along the Bay northward.

Photography by Shangle Photographics

Zabriskie Point, Death Valley National Park

The snow-dusted peaks of the Panamint Mountains and the foreboding Funeral Mountains, framing the vast desert lands below, punctuate the forlorn landscape of Zabriskie Point. As part of Death Valley National Park, Zabriskie Point provides an opportunity to appreciate the vast variety of what Mother Nature has provided. There are two genuine ghost towns in the Panamint Mountains. Panamint City is located in the northern Mojave Desert and the town of Ballarat is located in Panamint Valley, east Inyo County. The National Park Service states that the Park" is made up of 3,336,000 acres," of which 3,000,000 acres are wilderness area.

Photography by James Blank

Lower Twin Lake, Sierra Mountains near Bridgeport

Besides being located in one of the more beautiful locations in the Sierra Mountains, Lower Twin Lake is teeming with fish just waiting for the sportsman to drop the hook. This entire area is steeped in things to do and places to go. Fishing is good in Walker River and Buckeye Creek. Bridgeport Lake north of the town is a good fishing site as well as a camper's haven. Explore the canyons, old towns and historic buildings, and take time to tour the historic roads of the area, weather permitting.

Photography by James Blank

53

Castle Crags State Park, Shasta-Trinity National Forest, Northern California

These craggy peaks reach heights of 6,500 feet and are part of the Castle Crags Wilderness established in 1984. This special section of the forest was set aside for Castle Crags State Park, created by 4,350 acres. There are several miles of hiking trails and excellent camping facilities. The Sacramento River runs through the Park, providing an opportunity for swimming during those hot summer days so frequent to the area.

Photography by Shangle Photographics

Fort Ross State Historic Park, Sonoma County, Northern Pacific coast

California created Fort Ross State Historic Park in 1906, preserving this historic site and insight to the Russian settlement of 1817. The establishment of the Russian fort near Bodega Bay and about sixty-miles north of San Francisco instilled fear of invasion in the hearts of the padres of Mission San Francisco de Asis, threatening the strong position the Spanish had established in California. Besides being a mission built to provide medical care for the ill of Mission San Francisco de Asis, some believe Mission San Rafael was established as a buffer to potential trouble with the Russians.

Photography by James Blank

Historic Carson House, Eureka

Eureka, the largest north coast town in California, is filled with Victorian homes of the New England pioneers who settled the coastal towns in the 19th –century, giving it a look of transplanted New England. The William Carson House, built by successful businessman William Carson in 1885, is an example of the extravagant decorative urge of the time. Established as a gold-rush supply center, Eureka was also strong in the dairy industry in the 1850s and is still deeply involved with the industry. Deep-water Humboldt Bay has been an added advantage to Eureka's success.

Photography by Robert Shangle

Trinidad Head Lighthouse, Humboldt County, Northern California

The site for the lighthouse at Trinidad Harbor was established in 1866 and by 1871 the light became operational, as it is today. Built on a stone foundation, this white brick structure has a tower height of twenty-five-feet, rising a total of 196 feet above the harbor known as Trinidad Bay. The small town of Trinidad beckons visitors to its tranquil setting on the bluff overlooking the Pacific Ocean and Trinidad Bay discovered by Portugese explorer Sebastian Rodriguez Cermeno in 1595. Two Spanish explorers, Hezeta and Bodega, rediscovered the bay in 1775 and named it *La Santisima Trinidad.* The area was plentiful with fur-bearing otters in the 1800s. When gold was discovered in 1849, Trinidad became a supply port for miners. Trinidad Bay was a shipping center for the lumber industry and a center for fishermen. Tourism is an important part of Trinidad today.

Photography by Robert Shangle

The Founder Tree in Humboldt Redwoods State Park, Northern California

An organization titled Save-the-Redwoods League provides excellent information regarding the Redwood trees. Their efforts have preserved the mighty tree for the country and its people. Save-the-Redwoods League states, "California's magnificent Coast Redwood is the world's tallest known tree and one of the world's oldest trees. Average mature trees, several hundred years old, stand from 200 to 240 feet tall and have diameters of 10 to 15 feet, and some trees have been measured at more than 360 feet. In the most favorable parts of their range, Coast Redwoods can live more than two thousand years."

Photography by James Blank

Fisherman's Wharf on Monterey Bay, Monterey

Pleasure craft are tied securely to walkways and piers in historic Monterey Bay. The original wharf was built in 1846 for the purpose of handling the incoming trading vessels that maneuvered around Cape Horn. Sport fishing and commercial fisheries are prominent off the Monterey shoreline. Once the center for sardine packing, Monterey prospered for over fifty years, canning the small silver fish. Fisherman's Wharf was the site of the first major canning facility in Monterey, but it wasn't long before competitors appeared and opened quarters in an unimproved area near Pacific Grove, creating a road edged with fish canneries beginning in 1902. Author John Steinbeck's book *Cannery Row*, published in January, 1945, brought much attention to the road, and in 1953 the road named Ocean View Avenue was changed to "Cannery Row", honoring John Steinbeck. Many factors contributed to the demise of the canning processing in Monterey such as lack of fish, perhaps brought about by pollution and the use of the sardine in other forms of production.   *Photography by James Blank*

59

Mono Lake and Tufa Towers, Mono Lake Tufa State Reserve, East-central California

Being a geologist is helpful in understanding the production of Tufa Towers. Mono Lake is a non-draining body of water, therefore water evaporates leaving the salts and minerals that have reached the lake via intake streams from the eastern Sierra Mountains. Mono Lake is "2½ times as salty and 80 times as alkaline as the ocean" according to the California State Parks. "Tufa Towers are calcium-carbonate spires and knobs formed by interaction of freshwater springs and alkaline lake water." There is much to do and see in the State Reserve and surrounding area. A buoyant swim is an interesting experience in the lake water, plus hiking, boating and in the wintertime, cross-country skiing is on top of the list.

Photography by Shangle Photographics

Marriott's Desert Springs Resort, Palm Desert

So much beauty with the help of "just a little water," that is Palm Desert, and Palm Springs as well, plus all of the other small communities that have taken rise over the years. The desert locale has burst as a flower in the middle of the dry lands of California, with the help of "just a little water" and ingenuity from entrepreneurial minds. Influenced by the Southern Pacific Railroad property rights, available land owned by the Agua Caliente Indians, and the medicinal rewards gleaned from the clear desert air, Palm Springs was a "bound-to-happen" city. Hotel accommodations became a reality in 1886 and the need for more has been the impetus to many resoundingly beautiful resort facilities, created to reward those who "know what they really need", a special place to *flee away to*. These desert oases are unique in their very existence.

Photography by James Blank

Vineyards in the Napa Valley, Napa County, Northeast of San Francisco

Napa County is devoted to the culture of the grape and the production of some of California's fine wines. The rolling hillsides and terraces along with the warm mild climate are ideal for the growing of fruit particular the grape. Consequently this region has the highest concentration of wineries. Row after row of vines cover the undulating landscape like tufts of a blanket, adding their fresh green texture to the scene when their foliage emerges in the spring.

Photography by James Blank

The city of Los Angeles, Southwestern California

Hoping to attract settlers to the area, Felipe de Neva (the first Governor of California) circulated the word through northern Mexico that he was offering "free land, horse, and farm animals, a plow and other tools, and ten dollars per month in wages" for men of the soil. His generosity drew eleven men to a newly chosen pueblo site a short distance west of Mission San Gabriel. On September 4, 1781, the men and their families gathered around the site to witness a blessing of the lots by a San Gabriel padre. The name given was *El Pueblo de Nuestra Senora La Reina de Los Angeles* — The Town of Our Lady, the Queen of the Angels. Indeed, the small pueblo has flourished. *Photography by James Blank*

Joshua Tree National Park, north of the Salton Sea, South-central California

Unique to the extreme, Joshua Tree National Park provides something new and different for the average park explorer. Two deserts are located within the boundaries of the park: the Colorado and Mojave. As seasons change the vegetation makes its appearance with enticing delight, drawing visitors to explore the secrets of the desert. At one time plants were removed for personal use, but no more. In 1936 the Joshua Tree National Monument was created to protect the natural wonders of the desert. Since that time Joshua Tree has become a Biosphere Reserve in 1984, and on October 31, 1994, President William Clinton established the Joshua Tree National Park "as part of the desert protection bill."

Photography by Shangle Photographics

reminiscent of those times. The town was the site of large scale dredging operations at the turn-of-the-century, when many millions of dollars in gold were recovered. During this time the town itself was threatened with relocation in order to get at the gold bearing gravel thought to be under it. Like some of its sister towns of gold hunting days, Oroville has become tourist oriented, but its geographical situation may have had more than a little to do with this. It is considered the gateway to the Feather River Country, a major part of which is the forested canyon created by the North Fork of the river as it rushes down from high in the Sierra. The river is paralleled by State Highway 70, which eventually climbs over the range and down the eastern side. The Oroville area has other distinctions, too. It has become a fruit-and-olive growing region, its warmth having made this possible. In 1968 the Oroville Dam was completed and the water of the North, Middle and South forks of the Feather River filled the gigantic reservoir created by the dam's presence. The dam is one of the highest in the country. It is believed that the river was given its name by a Spanish explorer after he saw feathers floating on the lower river during a migratory flight of band-tailed pigeons.

The more remote heights of the Sierra are still very much the same untouched country as when the Native Americans had California to themselves. The millions of mountain visitors every year stay in the lower elevation, as a rule. What is called the High Sierra, mostly south of Yosemite, is alpine wilderness with no roads across it and only a few penetrating its lower slopes. Here is where the glacial scouring is most obvious and the glacial lakes most numerous, having more than 1,200 of them. The biggest peaks of the entire Sierra occur on this southern arm of the range, all of California's 14,000-foot Goliaths except Mt. Shasta and White Mountain. It is not forest or waterfall country, but it has a myriad of rushing streams moving down the slopes in cascades and rapids. The small glaciers that still remain are remnants of a comparatively recent period of cooling, not from the glaciers that covered the range during the Great Ice Age.

The unique personality of the High Sierra is manifested in what the glaciers left after they completed their work. The glacial-polished rock is an example. The light color and clean lines of these granite formations give the High Sierra a distinction among the great mountain masses of the country. Kings Canyon National Park, or rather parts of it, seems to fulfill in high style the requirements for a High Sierra landscape. Its jewel-like lakes are pure and austerely beautiful in their haughty, high altitude glacial fortresses. The John Muir Trail, longest in this part and in the contiguous Sequoia National Park, is the way into this enchanted world of shimmery blue lakes and stark, sharp ridges.

The John Muir Trail connects the three big parks of the Sierra, beginning at the edge of Yosemite National Park, the most popular of all the parks, going south into the other two parks. After 212 miles it ends on the highest Sierra peak, Mt. Whitney.

There is hardly a need to list the attractions of Yosemite National Park. Its waterfalls, deep chasms, and granite monoliths have been photographed and visited by many inquisitive tourists. But a short description is in order and it should start with the seven-mile Yosemite Valley itself. At nearly 4,000 feet in elevation, the valley is a glacial gorge with sheer walls rising 2,000 to 4,000 feet above a wide, flat floor something like a meadow. The cliffs of Yosemite beget a spectacular array of waterfalls. The highest of them is Yosemite Falls, dropping 2,565 feet in a series of tumbling and free-falling cascades. Yosemite's beauty and majesty are further displayed in such features as Mirror Lake, El Capitan, Cathedral Rocks, North Dome, Half Dome, and Three Brothers. For the ultimate in overlooks, there is Glacier Point rising 3,254 feet above the valley. From here the visitor can see a great deal of Yosemite spread out far below, with the silvery Merced River appearing trickle sized as it winds through deep green forests and open meadows. It is hard to believe that such a small appearing stream (with some help from glaciers) cut this fantastic chasm into the Sierra. From the available viewpoint, the clear air reveals in bold detail the complex features of the granite Sierra peaks that tower above the rim of the valley.

Yosemite is really two major canyons, the familiar one of the Merced River and a smaller, more northerly one called the Grand Canyon of the Tuloumne, or Hetch Hetchy Valley. Tioga Pass road runs along the divide between the two river drainage areas. Startling vistas of both Yosemite and Hetch Hetchy open up to travelers along this road. If combined, Sequoia and Kings Canyon National Parks are almost as big as Yosemite National Park. Kings Canyon is less accessible to visitors because of its high Sierra elevation, and penetration by road is limited. Kings and Sequoia parks are for the visitor who prefers their nature experience unleavened by fancy visitor accommodations. Some of the primary attractions are notably the Big Trees, *Sequoiadendron giganteum*. Giant Sequoia National Monument came into existence in April, 2000. The Sequoias are native only to the western slopes of the Sierras. (Their closest relatives, the coastal redwoods *Sequoia sempervirens*, are not quite as massive and grow in the northern California coastal belt). The bark of the Big Trees is cinnamon red with shades of gray. Over a long life that may span several thousand years, they reach heights above 250 feet, attaining an average diameter of 17 feet. Most of the Sierra Sequoias occur in the middle and southern parts of the range, with the biggest trees reserved for Sequoia and Kings Canyon parks. Some of the groves are readily accessible by car or by a short trail hike.

The survival of the Big Trees in the face of human settlement and the exploitation of the trees has probably been as much because of their relative inaccessibility as to the natural human desire to spare something so magnificent. Although the Generals Highway winds through some of the redwood groves, other stands of Sequoias are out of reach of many visitors, because they grow in the park's interior away from the highways. The far-eastern part of Sequoia Park, above the Sequoia belt, is comparatively unvisited. It has been compared to the spectacular glacial landscape of Kings Canyon and the higher Yosemite terrain. Its High Sierra environment either includes or is ringed by many of the tallest peaks in California, Mt. Whitney among them.

Lake Tahoe and the Lake Tahoe Basin, the other big and famous Sierra California treasures, are extremely popular with vacation goers and sightseers. This is a physically remarkable area, boasting of the lake, of course, and mountains, forests and high country valleys of exceptional beauty. The surrounding country contains both wilderness and developed-recreation areas. Squaw Valley, a few miles to the west, has been in the ski business since hosting the 1960 Winter Olympics.

Lake Tahoe is 22-miles long and extends to a maximum of 12-miles wide. It is one of the deepest of the glacial lakes and the surface of its intensely blue water is at an altitude of 6,225 feet. High up on the Sierra slope, walled by giant Sierra peaks raising snowy granite spires 3,000 feet and more, Tahoe has one of the more theatrically impressive settings of any lake. In summer the blue water is obscured with various colors from the swarms of pleasure craft, water skiers, and even swimmers; the latter limited to the state park beaches of the southern end, such as Emerald Bay, where the water is warmer. Winter visitors to Tahoe enjoy comparative seclusion, summertime being the period when most visitors appear. The winter snow season brings with it the risk of road closures around the lake. The Donner Pass area of the Sierras, which includes Tahoe, receives some of the heaviest snowfalls of the entire range, and blizzard conditions may block access to the north and south routes.

Central Valley

Even California is not quite an all superb vista of stupendous landscapes. If there is one part of the Golden State that is not so razzle-dazzle as the rest, it is the Central Valley. But even though it is not a winner in scenic sweepstakes, the Central Valley (sometimes the name is prefixed by "Great") does not apologize for its workaday aspect. The long, narrow basin is surrounded by spectacle. The curved-like mountain wall is nearly an unbroken boundary. The northern edge of the Central Valley is the Coast Range; the west and northwest edge is the Cascade Range, while on the south the Sierra's westward curving Tehachapis Mountains mark the southern end of the valley, by coming together with the coastal mountains south of Bakersfield. Finally, in the west the various titled coastal mountains intercede to keep the boisterous Pacific Ocean from kicking sand into its face. The only breach in the fortress around the Valley opens where the Sacramento River turns west into the Delta country behind San Francisco Bay.

The business of the Central Valley is agriculture and without the valley's production, California would not be the country's foremost farm state. From Redding in the north to the Grapevine ridge south of Bakersfield, it occupies a 450-mile trough that averages 50 miles in width. Strictly speaking, the Central Valley is not one but two valleys. The northern portion is named the Sacramento Valley, after the big river that drains its entire length. It reaches south to the Delta region around Lodi. South of Lodi the San Joaquin Valley takes over. The San Joaquin portion (also named for its primary river) is a great deal longer and somewhat wider than its northern counterpart, but it has much less drainage volume. The summers in the two valleys are about the same: hot. Winter in the northern valley is colder and much wetter than the southern valley. One result of this is a lavish stream runoff that is capable of making the mighty Sacramento River a little too mighty for comfort. The less impressive drainage of the San Joaquin River can be attributed not only to lighter rainfall but to the lack of any drainage to the ocean whatsoever in the valley's southern extremity.

The Central Valley's farm economy is based primarily on fruit orchards, vineyards, and staple crops. The cities of Sacramento and Stockton have become inland seaports, thereby making ocean access easier for the valley's products. When irrigation was introduced, orchards, citrus groves, rice and sugar beets surpassed grain production in importance to the region.

It is something of a surprise to discover that this 25,000-square-mile "breadbasket" of California and the world contains only about 15 percent of the state's population. The eastside of the Sacramento Valley is lined with communities that began as gold camps in the Sierra foothills. The towns haven't changed location other than by spreading their exterior boundary, but today their attention is on the green riches of the agricultural valley rather than the gold wealth hidden in the hills. The Feather River Valley towns of Oroville, Marysville and Yuba City now sit in the midst of northern California's most productive farmlands. The Feather River plain south of Oroville is an especially productive area for peaches, olives and oranges.

The primary river of the northern valley is the Sacramento. A considerable length of it is a natural, almost wild river, from about 50-miles upstream of Sacramento north to its source in the Trinities. Although the river runs through lowlands from Red Bluff to the Delta, its current is strong. Its banks and waters are gathering places for wildlife communities, and fishing is good. Overlapping migrations of salmon and Steelhead make the sport of angling rewarding for most of the year. The river is navigable at least as far north as Red Bluff, one of the many towns along the length of Central Valley that was started by gold seekers. Red Bluff's settlers never made it big in the gold business; they turned instead to the waters of the Sacramento to help them grow their wealth in the form of wheat and grapes. Some handsome old buildings remaining from the town's Victorian beginnings stand as evidence that the land yielded in abundance.

The Delta lands mark a vague boundary between the northern and southern valleys. The Delta is contained approximately within the rough ellipse formed by Sacramento on the north, Stockton on the south, and Antioch to the west. The two big river — the Sacramento and the San Joaquin — and some smaller ones come together here to form a lowland network of channels and waterways, with expanses of muddy land in between. The region was that of an everglade, low swampy land, heavily forested with oak and pine. The trees became firewood for the boilers of early river steam-powered boats, and the Delta became open marshland. Fertile and moisture-holding peat soils of the Delta Islands that hold nearly yearlong warmth have been orchestrated to produce money crops of asparagus and fruit. The deep Delta channels serve as waterways for both commercial traffic and pleasure craft. The levees that make crop growing possible on the low-lying land give the region a resemblance to Holland.

The San Joaquin portion of the Central Valley has been a relative latecomer in agricultural exploitation and population growth. Most of the explosion in crops and people has come about since World War II. Nearly all of the big towns, Stockton, Modesto, Fresno, and Bakersfield, and the smaller towns too, are massed on the eastside of the valley. The western valley was range country in the past and it is still used mainly for grazing. The wandering San Joaquin River and its tributaries have chosen many different routes to flow north, thereby leaving a network of sloughs over the land, and leaving reed-covered marshlands and abandoned channels. Winemaking is a big business in the San Joaquin region, just as it is farther north. Although the Napa and Sonoma valleys possess greater numbers of wineries, the vineyards in this southern valley are champions in volume. Fresno and Lodi are centers of wine districts where grapes are brought to peak sugar content by the long, warm summers.

The San Joaquin Valley is a working region before all else, but it has its contemplative moments. Strung out along State Highway 99, the road that connects the valley cities, are state parks, campsites, and recreation areas developed around lakes. Bakersfield, at the southern end of the basin, sprawls along the Kern River. The river supplies irrigation water to parts of the valley farther north, and it also runs out of a canyon of exceeding beauty and grandeur. The canyon, cutting into the Sierra ramparts, made Bakersfield one of the latter-day Mother Lode towns. Gold was discovered there in 1884, a little later than the gold frenzy that gave explosive birth to places up the valley. But its gold binge was equally wild and rough. Most of the original town didn't survive that brief era, succumbing to fire in 1889. But Bakersfield discovered oil too, in 1889, and until we learn to run our cars on something else other than oil products, that commodity will be more precious than gold.

Fresno is the big city of the San Joaquin Valley. Its size is directly related to its central location between the two California population concentrations, the Bay Area and the southern coast area. Fresno is, before all else, the headquarters of the agricultural activity all around it. But it is also admirably situated as a gateway to the beautiful recreational areas of central California. Lakes such as Millerton to the northeast are within a short distance. Not much farther into the Sierra wonderlands are places such as the redwood groves of the Sequoia and Kings canyons. The state highways reach them in short order from the Fresno area. The point for discussion is that Fresno, Modesto, Turlock, Merced and other towns located up and down the valley are the primary players in a bigger drama. They are surrounded by lush farmlands that produce in extravagant abundance throughout a long growing season. And their valley, while not a photogenic marvel like some of California's scenic treasures, has only to look up at the enfolding mountains around its fertile fields to feel an identity with them.

Desert Lands

Some of the world's deserts are being inhabited more than they used to be. Where nearby water makes human habitation possible, people are invading sandy, alkaline wasteland where rain seldom falls. Big cities and good-sized towns have appeared over time in the midst of desert land or on its periphery, such as Phoenix, Arizona and Las Vegas, Nevada, along with Palm Springs, California. People have gathered in these places by choice, to live in the arid climate and pure desert air that is touted as an elixir more potent and curative than any medicinal combination.

California's deserts are no exception to the process that seems to be giving dry spaces a better press than formerly. Palm Springs, camped more-or-less bravely on the northwest edge of the Colorado Desert under the steep shanks of the San Jacinto Mountains, is not alone. Now there is a group of desert tourist towns around it in the canyons, edging the Coachella Valley. That the Coachella Valley should be one of the world's most prodigal producers of grapes, dates, melons, and vegetables surprises no one any more. The bigger Imperial Valley to the south, right in the heart of the desert basin, is even better known for the abundance of its farm produce.

It is no secret that the desert will bloom when water has touched it. Lavish displays of spring wildflowers carpet desert canyons and flats after a winter of sufficient rain. The Colorado Desert occupies a triangle of land located in southeast California and is found to be one of the hottest, driest deserts anywhere. But it is also near reliable sources of water, primarily the mighty Colorado River. The fault-block mountains located on the west side, the so-called Peninsular Ranges, furnish ground water. Irrigation, combined with fertile alluvial soils, has transformed portions of the Colorado Desert into one of the most agriculture-intensive parts of the earth's surface. What remains is still an extreme desert land, defying man's ability to live in it with any permanent basis.

Deserts usually do not come equipped with lakes, especially lakes with water in them. However, in the middle of the Colorado Desert is the Salton Sea, a surprising phenomenon. The Salton lies between the Coachella and Imperial valleys, with a surface altitude of 235-feet *below* sea level. Everything in the lowly desert drains into this low-lying body of water. Nature may have more than once put a sea in the same spot, but the Salton is not one of them. A flooding Colorado River that burst through irrigation canals created it just a wink-of-an-eye ago, geologically speaking, in 1905. The sea is very salty due to evaporation and because it receives the salts drained by irrigation water from the farming valleys on the north and south.

The Salton Sea is big, 30-miles long and as much as 14-miles wide. In addition to its utilitarian function as a receptacle for agricultural drainage water, it has become a recreational lake and a wildlife sanctuary. Especially in the winter when temperatures are mild, desert-dwelling birds share its waters and shores with various other birds of passage. The northern and western edges even have some resorts, where fishermen put out with hook and line in search of the salt-tolerant fish that have been planted in those briny waters. One suspects, however, that the ultimate pleasure in visiting the Salton Sea comes from gazing at those expansive desert horizons stretching in all directions, while being rocked on the waves of quite an unlikely sea.

The Anza-Borrego Desert State Park west and south of the Salton Sea occupies a large portion of the dramatic desert vista. The "empty desert" theme certainly cannot be applied to Anza-Borrego. Its various terrains go from near sea level up to and beyond 6,000 feet. The State

Park covers a half-million acres and has been called the finest desert preserve in existence. Its protected status is vital and this part of Southern California in particular are being used more heavily than ever during the cooler seasons of the year. True desert lovers realize the fragility and interdependent structure of the desert ecology. But not everyone who comes into a desert wilderness from the land of buildings and pavement is willing to adapt. Vehicles, such as dune buggies and motorcycles in off-road desert spaces, have damaged some areas of the Mojave Desert and the Anza-Borrego. Vehicles easily damage fragile desert plants, for which ordinary survival is a tensely balanced struggle.

The huge Anza-Borrego reserve is ideal for the visitor who wants to explore the remote desert, the part that is out of the reach of roads. Roads, of course, penetrate the areas to some points, especially the nearer ones such as the palm oases in the canyons of the San Jacinto Mountains on the west. But some of the wilder regions of the park, as in the Santa Rosa Mountains of the north, quickly run out of even a suggestion of roads. In this ruggedly beautiful canyon and dry wash country, the backpacker-camper is king of the desert. Some of the lonely remains of gold miners' rock houses can still be seen in the Santa Rosa country's Rockhouse Valley. Places like these are beyond the determination of most people to reach them. The southern park precincts are equally authentic desert land, with a minimum of paved roads and other amenities. The canyons and washes, and the dry valleys within the folds of the Vallecito and Coyote mountains, still put a premium on resourcefulness, even though park rangers are constantly on the look out for anyone who has been put in peril by the beautiful and brutal world of Anza-Borrego.

Some of the hottest and driest places on the Colorado Desert are over on the eastern side. Yuma, in Arizona, is part of this hot and dry region that is sometimes called the Yuma Valley. Like the Coachella and Imperial valleys to the west, parts of the Yuma Valley are extensively farmed. Water is nearby and is taken from the Colorado River. The fertile soil of the delta area and a growing season that lasts year-round give it great productivity. This pocket of desert is bordered on the north by earth ridges such as the Chocolate Mountains and by the Sand Hills to the west. The Indians of the Fort Yuma Indian Reservation originally farmed most of the borderland. The reservation, which was established in 1884 with 48,000 acres, lost half of its northeast section to homesteaders. They now occupy the extreme southeast corner.

Joshua Tree National Park spreads over a transitional zone, separating the low Colorado Desert from the high Mojave on the north and east. Being thus situated, it has some affinities with both deserts. Its namesake tree dominates some of the higher ground, but it is not the whole show in this big desert preserve of 1,022,703 acres. The Joshuas make their stand on the open desert; palm trees, like the Washingtonia, are found in canyon washes. In the various altitudinal zones of the monument, the usual desert vegetation grows. Piñon pine, creosote, yucca, and cactus plants are distributed widely.

More than plants are preserved in a place like Joshua Tree National Park. The park is filled with creatures that find a desert a good provider. Not only are there foxes, coyotes, pack rats, squirrels, Jackrabbits, and mouse varieties, but bigger animals also loiter in the neighborhood. Bighorn sheep, badgers, and even bobcats make a living for themselves. And birds from the biggest to the smallest fly reconnaissance in search of desertfood. The large birds include Golden eagles and Turkey vultures; smaller ones are owls, roadrunners, and quail; the smallest are wrens and finches. The desert reptiles, tortoise, lizard and snake, are well represented too.

The National Park status was established in 1994, preceded by National Monument identity in 1936. Until recently the rarest species of animal within the Park was man. Now access by good roads around the perimeter makes it popular with more and more Los Angeles "refugees." Interstate Highway 10 on the south is a convenient escape route from the big city for them. The Park spreads from the mountains northeast of Palm Springs, about 60 miles into the eastern Mojave Desert. Joshua Tree is quite primitive, with very few amenities for visitors. Towns like Indio and Twentynine Palms, located on the highways to the Park are convenient launching areas for park exploration. Certain places inside the park are frequented more than other locations. The vegetation may be more abundant and colorful in one place over another, as in the Pinto Basin, a low desert region where Cholla cactus is widespread. Or the view may be one of the desert's most marvelous, as at Salton View, a highpoint where the desert panorama is endless and awesome at an altitude of 5,185 feet. From here the Salton Sea bids for attention on the south; tall and austere, San Gorgonio and San Jacinto peaks guard the western ramparts.

The Mojave

The Mojave Desert is California's biggest desert, located, as Californians say, in "East San Bernardino County." That is not exactly true but outside of a few tag ends that spill over the line in the west and southeast, the huge county does contain the desert lands, more or less. To add further definition, the Mojave makes up southeastern California, the part that is east of the southern Sierra and north of coastal Southern California. It is not really identified with the Great Basin deserts to the north, and most of it is within California. The high mountains of Death Valley and the other valleys directly east of the Sierra are more typically Great Basin desert, and most of that is in Nevada and western Utah.

Most of the Mojave is considered high country, between 2,000 and 5,000 feet. The average annual rainfall is two inches, a little more than the low Colorado Desert gets but not enough to keep it from being a full-fledged desert. It is cut off from moisture-laden Pacific storms by the continuous high ridge of the Sierra on the west and by the closely integrated mountain chains to the south. Its more mellow age is reflected in the comparatively gentle relief of its valleys and mountains. Innumerable basins are broken up by frequent low mountain ranges. The mountains were once much higher, worn down by erosion forces through eons of time, while ice-age lakes were occupying the desert valleys. For many people the empty Mojave Desert is a fearsome corridor located between the coast and the eastern border that must be crossed. It seems old and lifeless to the casual observer, but it is really neither. The Mojave is presumed to antedate the Great Basin lands, but for all that is comparatively recent in geological time scale. Ancient seas covered the Mojave Desert before it was raised up into highlands with steep mountains and deep canyons. Some of its many dry lakes had water in them about 500-years ago. Life is abundant on the land, although sparsely distributed on its arid plains and hills. The Mojave has even scattered examples of humanity living in areas east of Barstow all the way to the border, a total of about two-million or so acres between Interstate Highway-15 and I-40.

Barstow, safely connected to the mountain oases of the west by rail and road, takes a tentative step in central Mojave. The town was started in 1886 as a rail center and is still an important division point for the Santa Fe Railroad. Desert prospectors once used it as a starting point for the mining forays. Now Mojave visitors in search of something less tangible than gold begin their exploratory trips there. Some of the desert's finest efforts are within a short distance of Barstow. One of these is Afton Canyon, a gorgeous gorge to the east some 20 miles. The canyon is an oasis where the Mojave River that flows out of the San Bernardino Mountains on the west makes a rare surface appearance. Twelve miles northeast of Barstow, the ghost town of Calico has been restored to its former mining camp image. Some 20-miles farther north, at a mountain named Opal, Indian petroglyphs perpetuate the mystery of a civilization on the wall of Inscription Canyon.

Out on the east-central Mojave, where the roads and towns lose out to the overwhelming reality of the desert world, is a wild combination of mountain, canyon, and plain, under the jurisdiction of the Bureau of Land Management. Most of this area is under study by the BLM as a two-million-acre national preserve. The region has the contours of a younger desert, more so than the central Mojave has, along with an admixture of older forms. The high Ivanpah, New York, and Providence ranges are conspicuous examples of younger fault-block mountains. Nearby, Cima Dome's rounded top seems to announce one of the Mojave's more aged structures. The mile-high western wall of the sharp-edged Providence Mountains has the look of a mini-Sierra. High on the range is Providence Mountains State Park, one of California's most isolated preserves, and the site of Mitchell Caverns. The caverns contain evidence of ancient sea life embedded in the limestone, along with extravagant stalactite and stalagmite formations. The high park looks out on a long panorama of desert valleys to the south and east. Other dramatic variations on this eastern desert scenery are found at Hole-in-the-Wall near the caverns. Fractured mountains, lava flows, cinder cones and sand dunes make up a strange landscape that shows the effects of wind and water erosion.

The western Mojave is a very different desert, partly because of human labors. Antelope Valley, for example, with its advantages of nearby mountain water sources and greater rainfall than the desert's interior, has been turned into an agricultural basin. What helps is a built-in market just over the San Gabriel Mountains on the south: Los Angeles. A great portion of the valley is under cultivation but there is still some natural desert left over in its 75-mile length. Around Lancaster, the big town hereabouts, Joshua trees grow and the valley is a garden of desert wildflowers in the spring.

Death Valley

Death Valley National Park is the protective shield around a large region north of the main Mojave and east of the southern Sierra Nevada. Death Valley and the intervening valleys between it and the Sierra's east wall form a coherent region that seems to be of more recent formation than most of the Mojave. Owens Valley, right under the Sierra's wall, is perhaps not true desert, because it receives abundant runoff from the Sierra slopes, water that feeds the big Owens River, which in turn feeds the big Los Angeles Aqueduct. Owens Valley towns are gaining importance as headquarters for wilderness trips into nearby mountain regions, or out into Death Valley itself.

Death Valley is narrow in width and long in length, about 140 miles that is almost closed off by high mountains that rim the monument. The Panamint Range is the highest of these, topping off at Telescope Peak, 11,049 feet. They enclose the valley's west-side perimeter. The eastern barrier is formed, north to south, by the Grapevine, Funeral, and Black mountains. The rather severe statistics that cling most persistently to the valley's reputation tend to distort knowledge about it. The most remarkable facts are its extreme heat, aridity, and minus elevation. The record high temperature was reached at Death Valley's Furnace Creek in 1913: 134.6° F. Rainfall is usually one to two inches a year. And the lowest point on the continent, minus 282 feet, is at Death Valley's watering hole of Badwater.

More and more visitors are being attracted to Death Valley, especially in the cooler months of the year. Accommodations for auto travelers are limited and quickly become crowded, but hikers and campers have all the roaming space they desire. The main valley road, State 190, goes through the heart of the monument and touches some of its celebrated features. State Highway 127 north from Baker brushes the southern fringes of the Park, then continues north to connect with State Highway 190 at Death Valley Junction. Some secondary roads visit high viewpoints and get within easy walking distance of other highlights. The most visited sites are, predictably, the easiest to reach by car. From Dante's View in the Black Mountains, a wide panorama of Death Valley and beyond is revealed, including the lowest (Badwater) and the highest (Mt. Whitney) points in the contiguous United States. On the salt beds farther north below Zabriskie Point is an area of particularly grotesque mineral formations, including the Devil's Golf Course. Twenty-five miles farther north in the long valley, Satan is invoked again at the Devil's Cornfield, desert shrubbery forced into the configuration of corn shocks by wind and sand.

The Mesquite Flats Sand Dunes are one of the most striking features of Death Valley. They spread over 25-square-miles of the northern valley. Near the Sand Dunes is the village of Stove Pipe Wells, a man-made oasis for modern day desert travelers, built where one of the original water holes made the difference between life and death in early crossings of Death Valley. In the far north section of the valley, the half-mile-wide, 800-foot-deep volcanic cone of Ubenhebe Crater sits quietly. As volcanic activity goes, it is not considered very old, as the surface around it is testimony to fairly recent fire-and-brimstone displays. Nearby, through a canyon on the Grapevine Mountains that is breached by a side road stands Scotty's Castle, a provincial Spanish dwelling built in this unlikely location by a flamboyant fellow known as Death Valley Scotty.

The geological surprises and volatile, austere beauty of Death

Valley stir the imagination. This desert of many colors and textures becomes one thing and then another as the sun radiates different hues of daylight in its passage through the sky. Possibly the best place in Death Valley to see all of this is from the summit of Telescope Peak, that high perch in the western wall. The afternoon and evening hours are curtain time for the best lighting of this vary colored stage. But the visitor who aspires to reach this pinnacle must use leg and lungpower. It is six miles from the end of the road by trail to the top.

The Black Mountains supply the geological oddities, as well as a fair share of Death Valley's extravagant beauty. Even though these mountains are a young phenomenon, like the valley generally, they contain some of the world's oldest exposed rocks, figured at two-billion-years of age. They also exhibit vivid colors in the layered rocks at various points along their flanks. All of the mountains rimming the valley display streaks of rose, tawny, pale green, and so on. But the palette is most brilliant in the Black Mountains. These extraordinary mountains and all the other aspects of this unique desert seem to show us in their bare-bones intensity, the unity of all life and our true dimension as a part of it.

Scenic Coast

California has more than 1,000 miles of Pacific Ocean front-age, all of them gorgeous. In the north the coastal visage is rugged and dra matic. People are in a distinct minority and the smooth, sunny and populous beaches to the south have become symbols of a whole lifestyle. In between those two points, the California coast can equal or exceed the phenomena of any other state's coastline, excepting Alaska's icebergs, a shortage that causes no hardship.

The coastal spectacle is wild and highly dramatic in the north. California's northwest corner is a part of the Pacific Northwest and shares that region's propensity for rugged mountains, dense forests, and precipitous shorelines. At lands end the ocean slams against gigantic rock cliffs that plunge steeply into the foaming tide. Back of the thudding breakers, and sometimes right close by, are stands of coastal redwoods preserved in state parks, three of them bunched into the region north of Eureka. The world's tallest trees once made up a vast forest almost 500-miles long and 30-miles wide, from south of Monterey into the southwestern corner of Oregon. But even this vast gathering of trees represented a retreat caused by changes in climate and topography from the once-widespread redwood forests that grew in the Northern Hemisphere many millions of years ago. The more recent retreat of the redwoods to scattered groves along the northern coast was brought about earlier in this century, when the big trees were logged off as if there was no tomorrow.

As everybody's favorite road, the Redwood Highway (U.S. 101) wanders through the protected groves. It also offers some good views of the coastline itself, especially via segments of the old scenic roadway that has been bypassed by newer, four-lane thoroughfares. Scenic drives skirt the cliffs in some places, in the Crescent City vicinity for example and at little Requa, 19-miles south just off of the highway. The grandiose gorge of the Klamath River provides a majestic setting for the meeting of the big waterway with the Pacific.

Water in motion has not been kind to some of these coastal points. The flooding of the lower section of the Klamath River during the past years has removed parts or all of coastal settlements. The ocean waters have devastated Crescent City over the years, causing the town to be rebuilt, giving it a new look rather uncommon among the north coast communities. Its beautiful shallow harbor and crescent beach gain interest from the presence of offshore islands and rock structures.

The very special attraction of the north coast is preserved by the lack of exploitative development along most of its length. People are in the minority. Towns are infrequent and small, and their appearance usually fits in with the rugged grandeur of their surroundings. Even Eureka, the biggest north coast town, has a look of transplanted New England. Away from its downtown section, Eureka is filled with Victorian homes of the New England pioneers who settled these coastal towns in the 19th-century. The William Carson mansion is an extravagant example of the decorative urge of the time.

Eureka was started as a gold-rush supply center in 1850 providing materials for the gold miners. The reason it became such a busy place is close at hand — big, handsome Humboldt Bay. Even though the town is an emphatic presence on its shores, Humboldt Bay is much more than just a big, deep-water harbor. Beyond the harbor area, the 14-mile length of the Bay remains innocent of intrusive installations. The Humboldt Bay National Wildlife Refuge established on the South Bay in 1971 reaches up into North Bay too. Egrets and herons nest on the marshy acres of the bay's Indian Island, which is part of the refuge. Humboldt is the largest bay on the north coast after San Francisco, but it is well hidden from the ocean side by its two slender fingers of sand on the west side of the bay. Because of this it remained undiscovered long after other coastal features had been mapped. Its narrow outlet to the sea has in the past proved a treacherous passage for ships. Now long jetties provide a safer channel.

When one speaks of the rugged north coast, it is understood that the weather is one element in the ruggedness. Along most of its length, mist, rain and fog are more than just a sometime visitor. Often the rain drives in on the wings of a powerful storm that tears at the land as if intent on ripping it apart. At these times the Pacific Ocean seethes and crashes along the beaches or at the ponderous ocean side cliffs like a terrifying beast. Of some concern to sailors, the idea of a safe harbor takes on its deepest significance. Even in calm weather the coast looks ready to break loose, and no more so than on lonely Cape Mendocino, south of Eureka. The cape's big bulge carries the Coast Range right out to the ocean's edge along with it, except for the northern region south of Humboldt Bay. Here the precincts have long been lush dairy and sheep raising country. The cluster of towns in this valley is further example of the north coast's architectural preoccupation with the Victorian mode. Ferndale, one of these small communities, is filled with structures reminiscent of a bygone period with their charming and intricate Gothic carpentry.

But we were about to embark on an exploration of the mountainous Cape Mendocino Coast. The mountains of the King Range are among the tallest and steepest highlands on any coast. Their wild slopes afford marvelous sweeping vistas of the primitive coastline, an often-stormy tableau of sea-girt rock islands standing out of the angry waves, outlined in foam and mist. Sometimes, when the ocean is cloaked in fog, as it often is in summer, a ramble over the Kings' upper reaches will inspire a bittersweet sense of isolation for the wanderer. Thus transformed, the forests and meadows of the mountains become a magical, other dimensional world.

The long Mendocino (County) Coast begins south of Shelter Cove at the tag end of the King Range. The cove has a fine beach, interesting for its varied marine features, including rich fishing in the shallows around it. The northern part of the Mendocino area south of Fort Bragg is quite thinly populated, even though State Highway 1 (the Shoreline Highway) follows its indented profile closely. Relics of towns here and there are reminders of the early days of settlement, when lumber was more important to the coastal economy than it is now. Near Fort Bragg is MacKerricher State Park, particularly prized for its long beach, freshwater fishing and boating, tide pools and rocky outcroppings plus pine forests and meadows all in about 1,000 acres.

Fort Bragg itself is still very much a lumber town, although it now exerts itself on behalf of coastal fishermen and tourists. Proof of the latter effort is its status as the coastal terminus of the celebrated "Skunk" railroad that runs 40 miles east through the redwood forests of the coastal mountains to Willits in the valley. The trains take passengers on a thrilling and scenic journey over the high trestles and bridges of a logging railroad along the canyon of the Noyo River. The fishing activity of Fort Bragg centers on the Noyo River estuary south of town. A deep-water harbor there shelters swarms of fishing boats within its quiet confines.

Mendocino, the town, could with some justification be called the model community of the north coast for that look of old New England. Mendocino, however, is more than just a collection of old buildings. It closely complements its site on a headland 10 miles south of Fort Bragg. The townspeople, many of whom are artists and artisans, are concerned not only with preserving the look of a former era, but also with retaining the flavor of a less complicated style of life than we are accustomed to these days. A former lumber port, Mendocino has demonstrated an ability to keep out commercial development. State preserves that hem in the town help maintain the status quo. Mendocino Headlands State Park takes in the sea cliffs and the Big River beaches that border the town. Two miles north on the next headland is Russian Gulch State Park, from which the town can be seen across a wide bay. About the same distance to the south is Van Damme, another big State Park. This one is by Little River, in an area where a pigmy forest of cypress and Bollander pines is a curiosity. Van Damme is not a beach park, as it reaches five miles into the coastal hills, with one of those lush coastal fern canyons. The 40-mile piece of Mendocino coastline from Fort Bragg to Point Arena is blessed with three sizeable rivers; north to south find the Noyo, the Navarro, and the Garcia.

The big promontory of Point Arena furnishes yet another kind of coastal beauty. Here the coastal mountains stand back, leaving space for rolling pastureland, devoted to dairy herds. A tall lighthouse on the point with the coast's most powerful beacon completes the charming scene. Southward to Jenner about 54 miles there are few indications of human habitation except for a private "city" called Sea Ranch that blocks a long stretch of shoreline north of Stewarts Point. Stewarts Point is a ghost of a town, one of those tiny lumber ports of the past where ships were loaded by chute from land, often at the peril of all concerned when the seas were stormy.

Fort Ross still looks about the same as it did when the Russians were busy on the northern California coast, but that is only because it has been carefully restored as a state historic park. With the exception of the Point Arena vicinity, State Highway 1 has stayed close to the shoreline to get to this area. The beaches here are almost nonexistent, and approaches to them are difficult, both physically and legally as they are mostly in private hands. But the hardships of driving the snaky coastal profile and the limited accessibility of the ocean here is at least partially compensated for by the extraordinarily mild temperatures of this coastal stretch, with its many fog-free days as a further dispensation.

South to Jenner is another 12 miles, more steep, mountainous shoreline that forces the highway into repeated contortions as it negotiates high and narrow ledges overhanging the foaming surf of the Pacific Ocean. Things finally settle down when the Russian River is reached, with Jenner clinging to the steep slopes above it. From the Russian River to the Bay Area, the coastal backcountry becomes more crowded. Southern Sonoma county and Napa County east of the Bay Area are well furnished with towns and small cities. The immediate coast is still quite wild, although traffic pressure increases closer to the Bay Area. State Highway 116 at Jenner follows the Russian River into the redwood forests to one of the north coast's most popular resort and vacation areas. Guerneville is the centerpiece of all this, situated on the beautiful Russian River.

The Russian River is for most of its length a north-south stream, flowing in a long valley behind the coastal hills. This and other Sonoma valleys are, along with Napa County, devoted to the culture of the grape and the production of some of California's fine wines. The rolling hillsides and terraces created by the river's erratic course and a warm mild climate are ideal for the growing of fruit, in particular the grape. Consequently, this region has the highest concentration of wineries. Viticulture has added another dimension to the gentle beauty of the Napa-Sonoma countryside. Row after row of vines cover the undulating landscape like tufts on a blanket, adding their fresh green texture to the scene when their foliage emerges in the spring. The buildings of the different wineries exhibit a variety of architectures, blending unobtrusively with the fields of grapes around them.

Bodego Bay, south of Jenner on the coast, is Sonoma's only harbor. It is shallow, edged with salt marshes and tidal flats. Multitudes of invertebrates find it ideal for living quarters. Explorers of the beach and lagoon find ample opportunities for evicting clams and their kind from their dwellings. Bodega, the town, is an old-time fishing port, heavily used by fishermen who patrol the rich fishing waters of the bay vicinity. It has a shoreline of diverse environments congenial to a wide range of wildlife.

Below Bodega Bay the Shoreline Highway, defeated by the steep coastal cliffs between here and Tomales Bay, detours inland through a pocket of hilly wood and meadow country once farmed by the Russian colonists until they gave it all up in 1841. When the road wanders back to the coast, it is well into the shoreline of Tomales Bay, a narrow, warm water inlet on the lee side of magnificent Point Reyes Peninsula. Point Reyes is one of nature's most remarkable addenda to the California coastline. The wild, hilly promontory has been made into a National Seashore. Its vast dimensions encompass a variety of environments, from woods, meadows, and high, forested hills in the interior to seascapes in many guises — sandy beaches, steep bluffs, and rock shelves. Out on the point the weather is windy and foggy most of the time, but sunshine sometimes visits other parts of this peninsula. The ocean-facing beaches are uniformly stormy, but Tomales Bay, cutting down into the eastern base behind Inverness Ridge, beckons travelers who like warm water and sunshine to go with their sand.

Another of those scattered north coast redwood groves is near

Point Reyes, in the North Bay area. Muir Woods has been preserved as a national monument. Its lofty canyon wall does duty as an aerie for eagle-eyed observers who enjoy the sumptuous panorama of the Golden Gate and the Bay Area seen from here. The Muir preserve is the closest stand of redwoods to San Francisco, the apex of a glittering galaxy of communities that line the Bay shores. In the midst of such a great gathering of humanity, it is a special delight to have large areas of raw nature, such as Point Reyes, nearby. In addition to the big peninsula, coastal Marin County has other features where the natural values are undiminished. The coastal cliffs look down on beaches, such as Muir and Stinson, which are carefully maintained, providing close-at-hand nature experiences for Bay Area residents. Bolinas Lagoon, north of Stinson Beach, attracts a marvelous assortment of birds, including wide-winged ones like egrets and great blue herons, drawn by the abundant aquatic life in the lagoon's extensive mudflats. Most of the Marin County coast is now a public vacation land since the establishment of Marin Headlands State Park and the Golden Gate National Recreation Area.

The ocean side of the San Francisco peninsula is still quite rural, in contrast to the bay shore. After Pacifica, State Highway 1 rolls along the coast, unimpeded by towns for a while. Almost immediately it passes San Pedro Point, the high ridge where Spanish explorers got their first look at the big bay to the north. The road climbs over highlands above the point, opening up a wide view of the Bay Area and beyond to Point Reyes. Nearby, the gentle crescent of Half Moon Bay is the seaside aspect of an agricultural region where artichokes and brussel sprouts are grown in coastal valleys, where the weather conditions are just right: mild winters and cooling fogs in summer.

The shoreline profiles alternate sandy bluffs and pine-covered mountains down to Santa Cruz, at the northern end of Monterey Bay. Here the beaches are wide, white, and beautiful, with a boardwalk included. The town itself continues the Victorian architectural motif of north coast towns, but its outlook is modern, especially since the establishment in 1965 of a branch there of the University of California. South from Santa Cruz the state beach parks follows each other along the bay's wide arc like so many links in a chain. The country back of the northern bayshore specializes in the growing of fruit, especially apples and strawberries. In springtime the white blossoms of the trees and plants add fragrance and color to the fields.

The southern arm of the Monterey Peninsula is one of the world's climactic meeting places of land and sea. A benign weather regime goes with the dramatic confrontations of land and sea that characterize the peninsula's sometimes rock and cliff-lined edges. The temperature varies little — from the 50s° in winter to the 60s° during the summer. Fog hangs around on occasion, but there is generally an abundance of sunshine, even during the rainiest month, January. The town of Monterey is an embellishment to the beauty around it. Monterey's relaxed pace and the mellow look of its old Spanish architecture give the town a sense of continuity from the days when it was a Mexican enclave. The heart of the peninsula is the Del Monte Forest, a private preserve of exceptional beauty where wildlife may be seen but not hunted. The well-known peninsular 17-Mile Drive gives visitors an intimate glimpse of the forest's charms and passes by some of the peninsular beaches, touching Carmel Bay and Pebble Beach on the south. Carmel caps the peninsular landscape in its own relaxed fashion. The independent spirit of Carmel may derive in part from its attractive setting on the bay. The curving beaches are among the world's most beautiful.

Teeming offshore sea life adds another dimension to the beauty of California's coast. It occurs, of course, at many points, but at Monterey seems especially abundant. Offshore islands are so crowded with sea lions, seals, and sea birds that basking space is definitely limited. Even sea otters again patrol the near shore waters, after having been hunted close to extinction. At the southern end of the bay, Point Lobos has its share of visitors, both sea life and land life. The big, rocky peninsula has a road all the way out to the headland, with trails through pine woods to rocky perches where the various antics of the various sea creatures can be seen to advantage. For another 30–miles-and-more, the Big Sur coastline remains faithful to the wild and spectacular look. The coast highway clings for dear life to the steep shoulders of the cliffs that plunge toward the sometimes-violent ocean. The precipitous coastline is the forefront of the long Santa Lucia Range that crowds the central coast for many miles. The bleak Santa Lucia Mountains impart an air of mystery. They have a kind of Arabian Nights aura that achieves solid physical form in startling fashion about 40 miles south of Big Sur. There, on a majestic Santa Lucia eminence looking out to sea is a grand Spanish-Moorish *castle* known as San Simeon, a one-time home to William Randolph Hearst who created the Hearst publishing dynasty known throughout the world. It is now a state historical monument. A grander site for the elaborate estate could not be imagined.

Farther south along the coast road is Morro Bay, both the town and a bay, which is a pleasant stopping place. The community is on a bluff overlooking the landlocked bay or lagoon. The biggest piece of scenery in these parts is Morro Rock, a volcanic monolith that sits in the bay and reaches a height of 576 feet. San Luis Obispo, an historic mission town, is nearby. The Lompoc Valley just inland over the mountains some 40-miles south of San Luis Obispo is flooded with color a good part of the year. The long, rainless summers in the valley furnish ideal conditions for flower-seed growing. More than half of the world's supply of flower seeds is grown here. Between the towns of San Luis Obispo and Santa Barbara, the coast reaches peninsula-like into the Pacific Ocean. This considerable area is still sparsely populated, with just a few towns that could be called big sized. Vandenberg Air Force Base occupies a coastal tract, and the civilian part of this mesa land is dedicated to agriculture.

If San Francisco brings a certain tone to the north-central coast, then Santa Barbara might claim its own special contribution farther south. Like the fabled City of the Bay, Santa Barbara gets a head start in the beautiful-city sweepstakes by reason of its location. Its setting and climate are often compared to those of the Mediterranean's *Cote d'Azur*. The Santa Inez Mountains reach down to the coast and enfold the city in a natural amphitheater culminating in a small crescent bay. Santa Barbara's leisurely style of life seems appropriate in such a setting and with such a gentle climate.

The long chain of dazzling sandy beaches that stretch along much of the southern coast have become the most readily recognizable symbol of the California way of life. All over the world that combination of sun, white sand, and glorious surf has come to mean the good life. The lonely places are long gone, and the public beaches disappear under a human tidal wave on summer weekends. For getting away from some of this, there are the Channel Islands, most notably Santa Catalina, 27 miles out to sea from the Los Angeles beach communities. The resort town of Avalon is one of the few such places where tourists must leave their cars behind. Ferries to the island bring only people. The island's interior is a managed sanctuary for varied wildlife, with some supervised hunting. Nourished by the sea mists, the luxuriant vegetation of the island's valleys provides an attractive background for hikers and horseback riders.

Leaving aside the human artifacts that give Los Angeles its overpowering presence on the landscape, we can see that nature has provided a favored setting for this super city of some-hundred communities. The wide and long coastal plain has fostered the city's spread. The Santa Monica and San Gabriel mountain ranges, the lush San Fernando Valley, numerous canyons, and a long, long string of sandy beaches have given Los Angeles a marvelous variety of landscapes. In this rich combination of setting and climate, the Southern California state of mind — the belief that everything is possible —has been nurtured. One can hardly deny that it has taken such a belief to make the city a reality. Essentially a desert metropolis, it is sustained by marvels of engineering that bring water in huge pipelines from far distant points across the deserts that surround it.

The beaches south to San Diego seem to go on forever, a sort of sandy connection between the two arbiter cities of the Southern California idea. San Diego brings the Alta California coast to a glorious climax. A far more homogenous community than the City of the Angels, San Diego counts it days from 1542 when the Spanish and Portugese explorers (in this case Juan Rodriguez Carbrillo) were dropping in everywhere on the Pacific coast. A long time and many wars later, the settlement actually did become a city, incorporated in 1850. The city takes pride in her rich Spanish and Mexican heritage. San Diego is physically beautiful and climatically superb. Her good looks are keynoted by an enormous harbor that provides quiet waters for a worldwide maritime trade. The San Diego coast has more fine beaches than any other coastal stretch. The San Diego backcountry, too, is beautiful, moving from gentle rolling, pastoral landscape, quite untypical of Southern California generally, to mountainous, rocky terrain, but equally scenic. San Diego and its coastal kingdom close off the glamorous California seascape with a flourish.

California Missions

Title	Location
Mission San Diego de Alcala	San Diego
Mission San Luis Rey de Francia	San Luis Rey
Mission San Juan Capistrano	San Juan Capistrano
Mission San Gabriel, Arcangel	San Gabriel
Mission San Fernando Rey de España	Mission Hills
Mission San Buenaventura	Ventura
Mission Santa Barbara	Santa Barbara
Mission Santa Ines	Solvang
Mission La Purisima Concepcion	Lompoc
Mission San Luis Obispo, de Tolosa	San Luis Obispo
Mission San Miguel, Arcangell	San Miguel
Mission San Antonio de Padua	Jolon
Mission Nuestra Senora de la Soledad	Soledad
Mission San Carlos Borromeo de Carmelo	Carmel-by-the-Sea
Mission San Juan Bautista	San Juan Bautista
Mission Santa Cruz	Santa Cruz
Mission Santa Clara de Asis	Santa Clara
Mission San Jose	Fremont
Mission San Francisco de Asisa	San Francisco
Mission San Rafael, Arcangel	San Rafael

Oregon

California

California

*Mount Shasta

Redwood *
Nat'l Park

*Eureka   *Shasta Dam

Redding*   *Lassen Volcanic Nat'l Park

*Garberville

Mendocino *   San Francisco Solano
                (Sonoma)   *Lake Tahoe

San Rafael ✝
Napa Valley*   ✝ Sacramento

San Francisco ■ ✝   *Yosemite Nat'l Park
San Francisco
de Asis (Dolores)   ✝ San José   *Mono Lake
         ✝ Santa Clara
Santa Cruz ✝
Monterey *   ■ Fresno   *Sequoia Nat'l Park
San Carlos Borroméo ✝
(Carmel)   ✝ San Juan Bautista
Big Sur*   ✝ Soledad   *Death Valley
              ✝ San Antonio
              ✝ San Miguel   *Bakersfield
Morro Bay*   ✝ San Luis Obispo

              ✝ Santa Ines   *Antelope Valley
La Purísima ✝ ✝ Santa Barbara   *Joshua Tree
                                    Nat'l Park
Santa Barbara ■ ✝ San Fernando
San Buenaventura   ✝ San Gabriel
                                Anza Borrego Desert
           Los Angeles ■   ✝ San Juan Capistrano
Pacific   Long Beach*
Ocean   Newport Beach* ✝ San Luis Rey
                           ✝ San Diego
           San Diego ■

California

✝

California
Missions

Nevada

Mexico